Puppy Training

How to Housebreak Your Dog in a Week (7 Days)

Neil Doss

Table of Contents

Introduction 2

1. Understanding Your Puppy 5

2. The Growth Process of Puppies 12

3. Positive Reinforcement 19

4. Choosing a Crate 26

5. Training Equipment 29

6. Methods of Housebreaking 34

7. Housebreaking Do's and Don'ts 43

8. Putting Your Dog on a Schedule 47

9. Potty Training Process 50

10. Top Training Techniques 54

11. Cures for Behavior Issues in Dogs 64

12. Giving Dog Treats 72

13. One Week Formula of Housebreaking 76

14. Common Dog Training Mistakes 83

Conclusion 91

Introduction

We define a puppy as a juvenile dog between the ages of birth and one year, the point at which the majority of dogs have reached sexual maturity and thus adolescence. This book will focus primarily on puppies between two and six months old.

Age matters for puppies because they are operating within fairly brief developmental windows. It is only during the first few months that a puppy's brain is plastic, meaning that its connections are still being formed. The more plastic the brain, the greater the opportunity for a puppy to learn.

The majority of people get their new puppy around eight weeks of age. It is for this audience that this book is intended. If you have adopted a six-month-old puppy from a shelter or rescue who requires basic training, that puppy has likely suffered at least some neglect and will probably arrive with some behavioral and trust issues and attachment disorders. This book can help you deepen your understanding and can provide some helpful tips, but this book (or any book) is not going to suffice. You will benefit from the help of a professional trainer. Potty training a six-month-old is very different from doing so with an eight-week-old.

Beyond the owners of puppies of a certain age, who is this book for?

It is for first-time puppy owners and those getting a new puppy who would not mind a little refresher. It is for those who are committed to positive training and willing to exercise all the necessary patience and restraint to shelter their puppy from the inevitable frustrations you might feel. And it is for those who are willing and able to set aside the time and give the attention needed to properly raise and train a puppy. Throughout the book you will see reminders of the importance of attentiveness and supervision.

If your schedule is such that your new puppy is going to be home alone for more than a few hours during the day on a regular basis, we'd ask you to reconsider bringing a puppy into your home, unless you have a plan in place that makes liberal use of dog walkers, friends, or neighbors to fill in the gaps when you're gone.

We know that life can be full and busy. This book offers a training plan that will help you manage a life that includes this incredible new family member. And throughout, we will provide assistance on when and how to leave your puppy with thoughtful confinement, and also about how to take your puppy with you out into the world.

We know that every puppy owner wants to have a well-adjusted, emotionally stable dog who is friendly, happy, and able to serve as a super fun companion on many of your outings. And for that reason, we are going to emphasize the role of early socialization—and plenty of it—throughout these pages.

This book will provide you with everything you need to know to get your house ready for your puppy, to crate and potty train them, to socialize them, and to teach them basic obedience, all in seven simple steps. The steps themselves are easy, and your puppy will learn. But do prepare yourself for challenges—challenges to your ability to remain patient, consistent, and positive in the presence of juvenile rambunctiousness and wanton destruction. But we are going to be right there with you, every step of the process.

1. Understanding Your Puppy

Understanding Your Puppy's Behavior

In order to effectively bond with your new puppy, and have the best relationship possible, a basic knowledge of dog psychology is necessary, and understanding these basics will help you communicate with your dog on a deeper, and more meaningful level. Remember, when you first bring your puppy home, he will be in a strange new place, without his regular pack or littermates. You will have to show your puppy around and let him know that you will be taking care of him. Be patient, a new home can be scary for anyone.

Dogs need discipline as well as love. They look to their human companion for guidance through consistent discipline and effective training and can become confused and insecure without that guidance. Your puppy will be safer if you start obedience training early. A well-trained dog can be called away from a potential hazard and will not chase other people or animals when it is called to heel. Your puppy should also be socialized with other people and animals to be certain that it does not become aggressive to or fearful of strangers and new animals.

How a Dog's Mind Works

Realize that a dog will behave according to its breed. Herding dogs will always enjoy herding something, fishing breeds like to swim. Being aware of your dog's breed qualities will help you understand what instinctual behaviors your dog might be prone to and can help you satisfy the natural tendencies of your puppy in a healthy, constructive way. This being said, each dog has its own distinct personality, just like humans do.

Dogs have both short-term and long-term memories. They use their long-term memory to remember tricks, like "roll-over" and "sit". Their short-term memory can actually perform better when food is used to reinforce the memory. For a dog, memories are deemed more or less important depending on how helpful they are to their survival, according to their instincts. This is how they can remember that you threw away some bacon in a particular bin, so they will always go back to check that particular bin for bacon! Research has even shown that dogs can dream, possibly, similar to the way that humans do.

Dogs are capable of learning commands, recognition of certain nouns, verbs, and phrases, and can discern the subject matter of a command by following a gaze or reading the emotion behind your voice. Dogs can also exhibit other aspects of human psychology, such as being susceptible to disorders, like depression or anxiety, and compulsive behaviors. Our canine companions also experience emotions, such as fear, happiness, sadness, and even jealousy. They learn by watching their elders, or other older animals and mimicking rewarded behaviors, and will also mirror emotional cues from their owners in a social setting.

Dogs can understand what gets them attention, and how to use that information as a tool to elicit a reaction. Most dogs are on about the same cognizant level as a toddler, in fact researchers agree, they are usually on approximately the same intelligence and understanding level of a two-year-old. Dogs are capable of varying degrees of self-control, depending on factors such as temperament, training and breed. They follow social instincts handed down from their wolf ancestors, making them naturally good readers of body language and social cues, and they have evolved these skills to better read the moods of their human companions. Since dogs are unable to communicate verbally, they rely on facial expressions and body language for visual cues as to their human's moods. Dogs are also very good at recognizing vocal tones and inflections.

The scent of a dog's owner activates the reward centers in its brain, and one study by Dr. Gregory Burns, a neuroscientist at Emory University, shows that dogs respond about equally to praise and food. This study shows dogs love their owners at least as much as they love food, find pleasure in their company, and will go to great lengths in order to please their human companions. Dogs also see their humans as their safe, happy spot. Research into how our dogs think has shown that along with an owner's scent activating the reward centers in the dog's brain, our dogs have feelings for their owners similar to the way infants feel for their parents, they view us as a safe and constant presence, a secure foundation in the changeable, unknown, and sometimes scary world.

Studies show that our dogs love us as much as we love them; our dogs show us in their own ways, too. Some signs that your puppy pair cares for you are:

- Eye contact.
- Wagging tail.

- Snuggling/ cuddling.
- Sleeping with you.
- Bringing you toys.
- Mimicking- i.e. yawning when you yawn.
- Leans against you.

Dogs are the only animals that can intuitively understand human gestures such as pointing. They can understand basic math functions; if they have one treat and get another treat, they know they should have two treats. A dog's cognitive abilities allow it to learn new tricks, remember commands, and figure out just how its human is feeling by studying body language, facial expressions, and tone of voice. Our canine companions are much better at picking up short words and phrases than long ones, and most likely only listen to the first syllable or letter that we say. Dogs use their sense of hearing to process new words. When your puppy hears a new word, they will associate that word with the other new thing in their environment. Once an unfamiliar stimulus, or new word, is detected, the brain switches the learning centers on, in order to understand the new stimulus.

Physical and Mental Exercise

Now you know that your dog has a mind capable of learning, remembering, and basic problem-solving, but what you may not know is that your dog's mind will work best if you give it some stimulation. Keeping a dog's mind active with mental exercise is just as important as keeping your dog physically active, and there are a number of ways to do this. First, keep your puppy learning. Training your puppy provides him with mental challenges. Training is a mental exercise that can be continued all the way through your dog's life. We would not stop teaching a child to do things after it learned potty training, so why stop training your puppy? Once you have the basics, like sit, stay, and heel, under your belts, keep going. You can find lots of ideas for tricks to teach, or new commands to try, in order to keep your dog engaged in learning. New mental challenges can also keep your dog calmer, by alleviating boredom. Socializing your dog frequently will also provide positive stimuli. When your dog's senses are engaged meeting new people and animals, it will be more alert and better able to handle meeting new people and animals.

Dogs learn by repeating behaviors that attain good results, and not repeating behaviors with negative ones. While dogs do experience emotions such as contentment, anger, excitement, and love, experts widely believe they do not feel some of the more complex emotions like guilt and pride, or shame. If a puppy seems to be cowering with guilt and shame following to a mess he just made, it is more likely to be related to the fact that he's equating the mess with punishment, not the fact that he made the mess.

Often, when a dog is having a difficult time picking up new words during training, the human is giving a mixed cue, like lowering the head while giving a command. The dog hears the command to do one thing, but the body language says something else. When a dog follows a command, they are listening more to the inflection and tone of voice we are putting into that word or phrase when we say it than the actual command itself. Basically, they are reading the intention behind our words, based on the body language, emotional, and vocal cues they are given. This is why you can get a dog to "stand up" or "dance" with a high-pitched, baby-talk voice, but it's much more difficult to get them to calmly sit using the same voice. The best way to keep them calm is if you remain calm yourself, this way your intentions can be read in a relaxed and positive manner. Coupled with an innate desire to please their human companions, a dog's intelligence makes them eager and willing students who want to learn what we have to teach them, and by learning to communicate more effectively with our dogs, we can enrich their minds and train them to become a well-behaved member of the household.

If your dog seems restless, or if you have noticed some breed specific destructive tendencies, you can try and engage them in a game that satisfies their breed instincts. A retriever, for example, will likely be most satisfied playing fetch, and most terriers would like to tunnel. Find creative ways to get your dog doing a job it naturally wants to do. A fun challenge for you and your puppy is interactive games and toys. There are many toys on the market now that allow you to hide a treat inside, so that your dog can solve the puzzle of getting their reward for themselves. Memory and board games are even available, for a fun and exciting way to challenge and engage your dog's mind. Taking your dog with you as you run errands is also a stimulating experience for your puppy. Even a short trip to drop off mail, or to pick up some takeout will provide your dog with numerous new smells and experiences, and actually make for a calmer dog when you are finished and return home. Rotate toys to keep your puppy entertained. Once a new toy is brought into the home, let your dog play with it until they show less interest, then switch it out for either a new toy, or one that they haven't played with in a month or so. Your dog will be just as excited by the toy he has not seen in a month, as he will by a brand new one, and they will remain entertained by their toys longer this way.

Puppies need lots of exercise as they grow, and play time is important for your dog's development, health and happiness. Walking your new friend can be a healthy benefit for both you and your pet. Even if you are just walking around your yard, time spent outside just sniffing and exploring is a well-loved treat for your puppy. You can also try keeping some treats handy while walking your puppy, especially if you are still house breaking him. A small reward when "business" is done outside is a powerful incentive for your puppy that he will want to earn again.

2. The Growth Process of Puppies

Puppies begin to learn right after birth, so it is crucial to understand what is going on in those vital first weeks of existence.

Puppies learn several lessons from their parents and their siblings. Mothers have to wash the puppies so that they can urinate and defecate, and then they also wipe the pups clean. That is how the puppies figure out how to stay healthy. If they do not have this contact with Mom because they were taken away from her too early, they can have difficulty learning home-training afterward; this is also a concern for puppies purchased from pet stores.

Puppies cultivate bite resistance, which means that they do not bite too hard to play with their siblings. When the puppies play, if one hits another too hard, the receiver will yip or snap and stop playing. The chomping puppy might not want to stop playing, so he learns to reduce the severity of his bite. Puppies also learn bite resistance from their mother, particularly as she begins to wean them. Puppies are now learning to share with their fellow pups. They learn about resource rivalry, such as with toys or with their mother's milk. There are valuable social lessons that are crucial at this age, which is why it is valuable never to take the puppies away from their families too early. Good breeders and rescue groups will be holding puppies with their families for at least eight weeks.

If a mother dog has one puppy in the litter, called a singleton, it is at a disadvantage. He cannot learn bite avoidance very well because he has no brothers or sisters to show him when he bites too hard. This could prove to be a hurdle for you because the pup could be very mouthy. He never has to share or fight for something, so he may find it really upsetting when he unexpectedly does not get what he wants when he comes to your home. You are going to have to spend extra time teaching a singleton puppy.

Some people tend to have two puppies or young puppies at the same time. This is definitely attractive, as the puppies are going to spend a lot of time together and be playmates, but it may create a few problems. Puppies raised together may become overly reliant on each other because they spent their time together, particularly if they are packed together, so they do not learn to be alone. And when one of them has to go to the vet or gets to go somewhere without the other, the puppy left behind can become disturbed. Too much reliance is not safe.

Another problem is that as they spend this much time together, they are often more closely bonded to each other than to you or to other people in your family. Dogs are most closely bonded to someone who spends much of the time in meaningful interactions. When a puppy spends most of his time with another puppy in a vital socialization period, that is who he is going to be bonding with. You will probably find that they are not listening to you, particularly if they are older, which will make their training a bigger challenge.

Some littermates can also grow animosity towards each other as they get older. Often, aggression can escalate to a point where it is not healthy or safe to hold both pups together any longer, which is frustrating.

Raising young puppies together can be done, but it takes a lot of effort, time, and commitment. You will need to make sure each puppy has its own crate and bowl. You have to divide them every day for individual bonding time with you and other members of your family. You are going to have to train them separately and take turns on journeys and adventures. With all you need to do to get the puppy trained right, the extra effort may prove to be a bigger challenge than you are prepared to face. That is why so many professional trainers do not suggest getting littermates.

Reading Body Language

If you want to really understand what your dog is telling you, his body language will tell you all about it. Dogs have a dynamic, broad body language vocabulary; this is how they interact best with each other. Dogs know what a nice dog is doing, what it sounds like, and how it behaves. They even identify an enemy dog in the same way. Dogs indicate by their body language when terrified. By signaling with the body language, a dog may disperse a potentially stressful situation and stop combat. Through better knowledge of the body language of a dog, you can understand your dog better.

Eyes

A gentle, sweet smile suggests kindness or contentment. Your dog's eyes may be squinted. If your dog looks at you in a friendly or warning face, it is all right. Many people fear that if a dog looks at them in the eyes that it is a threat or a dog is simply showing itself. It is scarcely is! Your dog is probably only making friendly communication or trying to interpret your own language. Eye contact is a sign of boldness, which is not the same thing as hostility. This is why timid or nervous dogs often pull away from you.

Ears

When the ears of a dog lie flat, it can imply fear. Forward ears show curiosity or excitement. Remember that certain dogs have ears that do not give them a lot of speech. Cocker Spaniels, for instance, have stunning, long ears that normally lie flat and do not stand upright.

Mouth

Some dogs laugh, and that is exactly what you think it is — a sign of excitement. A tight, closed lip is a sign of stress. The lips can be drawn back at the corners. Depending on the situation, panting can indicate stress. A dog who has been playing is going to bark, so that does not mean it is mad, but a dog that's scared of thunderstorms is always going to bark when the storm starts. Dogs can pant if they are in pain. However still, if a dog is panting and closes its mouth, there may be an increase in stress. For instance, if a dog is breathing heavily at the vet's office and unexpectedly stops as the vet's technician approaches with the thermometer, the dog's stress has just intensified.

When a dog tells you or another animal to steer clear, his lips can move forward over his teeth to make them look puffy. His lips may even curl up in a snarl and withdraw to reveal his teeth; this may be followed by a groan. It is separates from a submissive smile, which is frequently mistaken for a snarl. In a submissive expression, the lips of the dog draw up vertically to reveal the front teeth. It is often followed by a subservient body posture — a curved back, a short, wagging tail, occasionally looking away, and squinty eyes.

Tail

The tail curled under is a symbol of terror. A wagging tail is frequently mistaken for a sign of kindness, but this may be a serious error. Just because a dog is wagging its tail does not mean that it is social or that it wants you to pet it. A tail that is very low and shaking quickly can give rise to stress or anxiety and can also give rise to excitement. The tail, which is held very high and wagging, shows high enthusiasm. The dog might be excited to welcome you, or he might be irritated and may contemplate lunging and even biting. Generally speaking, a mid-level or low, frilly tail wag is a symbol of joy or friendliness. Some dogs are so incredibly happy that their tails go flying around in wide circles.

A dog's overall body posture will tell you a lot about his thoughts and what he is feeling. A dog that puts most of its weight on his forelegs is attempting to increase the distance between himself and something. He may be confused or frightened. When his weight is positioned forward, he is trying to reduce the gap. He is curious or willing to do something. For instance, a puppy who is unsure of a tall man may lean backwards, away from a man. If he feels that the guy is fine, he is going to lean or step towards him. When a dog is tense, he is going to move his weight back and forth. At the same time, he may be scared but interested.

A curved body pose suggests friendliness or pacification. Many dogs appear to wiggle and wag with their whole body! When a dog lifts his paw, it can indicate peace of mind and could be an invitation to play. When a dog drops his head and bends his knees, but the back of the dog stays straight, this is considered a play bow. It is an open invite to play, and a way for a dog to show that it is not a threat.

When a dog drops his head, tightens his body, and puts on a hard-hitting "lock and load" face, his aim is to attack. It does not actually mean that the dog is going to bite, but it obviously wants you to leave. He could escalate to a bite if pushed. You can see the fur growing on the back of his neck or all the way down his back. This is called "piloerection."

How Your Dog Sees the World around Him

Like natural eyes, canine eyes comprise of cones and poles; be that as it may, there is an accentuation on their poles, while we have an accentuation on cones. Their accentuation permits them to find in obscurity and diminish light multiple times better than we can. The accentuation on human cones permits us to have a more prominent range of hues in brilliant light. We have three cones, while hounds have just two. In spite of prevalent thinking, they are not partially blind, however ready to decide different shades of violet, indigo, and blue, and perhaps red. They experience issues recognizing hues between green, yellow, orange and red. The shading blue green seems white or a shade of dark to them. In spite of the fact that our canine sidekicks appear to have less capacity deciding hues, they are in reality much better at separating subtler shades of dark than people are.

3. Positive Reinforcement

Why use positive reinforcement in dog training?

Training with positive reinforcement is rooted in the old saying 'You can catch more flies with honey than with vinegar.' Your puppy wants to please his alpha and using that as a training method makes life easier and much more pleasant for both of you!

Positive reinforcement rewards a dog for behaving in the expected manner but refrains from using loud voices or physical approaches otherwise. There is no real 'punishment' for bad behavior. Punishment is negative reinforcement. If it is not the desired behavior, it is ignored as much as possible. Attention, even negative attention, reinforces bad behavior. Treats, attention, and snuggling can only be achieved by giving the behavior that was desired by the alpha.

Let us take Mario and his puppy, Buddy, as an example.

Mario is an average guy. He adopted Buddy from one of the dog shelters near his neighborhood because he has always wanted a dog to call his own. One day, he decided that Buddy had to be trained. He tried a few methods of training before he settled on one that he felt was right and effective.

First, Mario tried to be the dominant, alpha male in his relationship with Buddy. Whenever Buddy would pull on his leash during walks, Mario would pull him back harder or would smack the side of Buddy's hind legs with his foot. If Buddy chewed on a shoe or a pants leg, Mario would make his disapproval known by forcefully taking the object away and scolding Buddy loudly. This resulted in Buddy being afraid of Mario.

While he did learn not to pull on the leash or chew on anything inappropriate, he also learned that his human companion was scary and could not be trusted completely. Buddy became jumpy and insecure. He would bark at other dogs and would shy away from other people.

When Mario saw how his training method was affecting his dog, he decided to try another way. He trained Buddy with a firm but gentle voice. He never laid a hand on his dog again, except to praise him, or carefully and slowly push or pull him away from a potentially dangerous situation. Mario focused his energy on praising Buddy every time he did something right and correcting him, instead of scolding him, whenever he did something wrong.

The effect on Buddy was immediate. He became eager to please and was no longer afraid of Mario. Buddy learned to enjoy his training sessions, as well as genuinely listen to Mario's commands. The bond between human and dog deepened and both of them became happier.

The story of Mario and Buddy is one that has been repeated again and again in homes where individuals are discovering the wonders and benefits of using positive reinforcement. Instead of punishing dogs because they are committing mistakes they do not fully understand, positive reinforcement asks dog owners worldwide to shift their perspective and focus on the good points of their dog's behavior.

There is a solid scientific basis to why positive reinforcement is very effective as a training method. Dogs are creatures of habit. They value routine and look for patterns in their day-to-day activities. They learn about their companions and environment in the same way a toddler or child does—by repetition.

This means that if a puppy is consistently rewarded for behaving in a certain way, he will continue following that behavioral pattern. Positive reinforcement is a humane and non-threatening way to teach any desired behaviors. It also shows puppies and dogs alike that their human family, and especially their alpha, can be trusted, and that prevents stress and helps them to feel safe.

Confidence, and not fear, is instilled alongside the good habits that form whenever an owner uses positive training methods. Canines are very intelligent and positive reinforcement makes them use that intelligence. They are challenged to figure things out and sometimes you can almost see the wheels turning in their heads. I well remember watching a little American Eskimo pup obviously thinking through the givens of the situation: pee outside, get treat and praise; pee in the kitchen, get ignored. He seemed to reach a conclusion, looked straight at me, and very deliberately started to pee on the kitchen floor. A firm calm 'No' and I whisked him outside, where his peeing in the grass was rewarded. Ears and tail went up and he pranced back inside, very pleased with himself. It was his 'Aha!' moment, and my floors were clean and dry for the following 16 years. He definitely 'Got it!' and was testing his theory!

Positive reinforcement is often paired with negative reinforcement, as in the example above, for speedy results. In the housebreaking situation, it would work like this. If I discover a puddle on the floor, I just clean it up. No words, no recrimination, no dirty looks at the pup, nothing. That behavior has been ignored. However, if I catch him in the act of making a puddle, I react immediately with a firm 'No' and an unhappy face. I grab him and move him as quickly as possible to an acceptable piddle spot. Any peeing there, no matter how little, is lavishly praised with a big smiling face. The pup will naturally prefer the smiling praise to the unhappy 'No'. Wouldn't you? I have reinforced the behavior from both sides, and I have made very clear what makes this pack leader happy.

It is important to note that dogs are very good at reading body language, so controlling your physical expressions is important. It is a natural form of communication for them. Dogs use ear and tail position, as well as whole body stance, to let each other know friendliness, challenge, willingness to fight, protectiveness, and pack position. Do not be surprised if your puppy goes belly up—the position of submission—when he meets someone or another dog. He is just acknowledging that they totally outrank him, and he accepts it! Make sure that your body language is positive in order to send him the correct messages.

Other desired behaviors can be achieved the same way. If sitting gets a smile and a treat and jumping up does not get anything, guess whose butt will start hitting the floor regularly! When you begin house-training, also begin teaching the basic commands, especially 'sit.' Make that pup sit to get a treat, sit to get his meals, and sit before playtime or petting. In a pack, nothing is free; rewards are earned. Be the alpha who demands and rewards acceptable behavior.

How to Use Positive Reinforcement to Train Your Dog

To start with, you should ensure that the treats are little, so they do not fundamentally add to your pooch's general every day caloric admission. Second, you should possibly compensate the canine when he effectively plays out the ideal conduct. Give your pooch the prize each time he reacts properly for the initial five or multiple times. At this point, your canine ought to have made the association between the prize and the conduct. After this point you can begin to eliminate the food rewards.

It is essential to eliminate the food awards after your canine makes the association between the conduct and the prize since you do not need him to get subject to the compensation to play out the conduct. When your pooch has its hang, begin to compensate him just every other time. You should keep on lauding your pooch for carrying on effectively and you can begin to offer a toy or a couple of moments of paunch scouring rather than the treat.

Establish Communication

Continuously state your canine's name decidedly! Never in a reproving tone. Whenever your canine reacts to you saying his name, regardless of whether it is basically taking a gander at you or coming to you, let him know "YES" and prize him. Along these lines, your little guy will start to learn right off the bat that consultation his name is a positive encounter that is ordinarily trailed by a prize (regardless of whether that is a treat, toy, or basically their proprietor's adoration and warmth)

Establishing that you are calling your dog's name as a positive thing is the first major step to establishing strong recall habits.

Afterward, when your dog is off leash and he starts to run after another dog, you are going to call him to come by his name:

"Rover, come!"

If, however, your pup's name is used in a scolding tone, he is going to look at you and think: "Am I in trouble, or am I getting a reward? I'm not going to chance it!" *Dog then bolts off towards another dog*.

Keep training sessions short and fun

Training is tough, but it is also FUN! To make this process less intimidating, you really need to have a good time with training—make it fun and short for both you and your pup. It will go much more smoothly and efficiently if you go into it with a positive attitude! Make training a fun and happy thing so that your puppy will get excited about it and look forward to it! Just remember that puppies have short attention spans, so do not get frustrated when your pup starts checking out. There is a reason I only offer my clients one-hour long training sessions: dogs do not typically have attention spans any longer than that!

4. Choosing a Crate

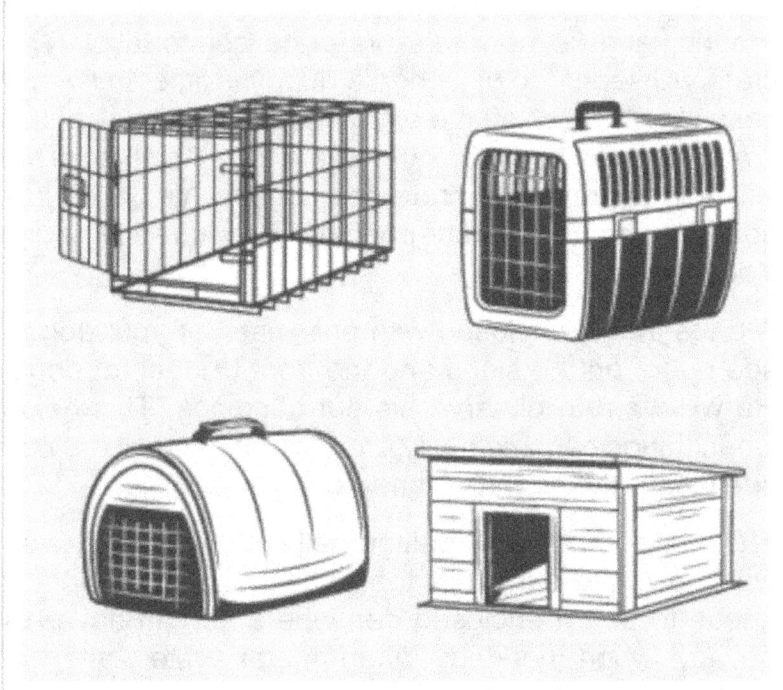

Dogs are inherently cave dwellers. They love having a den of their own. A dog crate can be a useful tool as well as a calming hideout for your dog. Your home is a great place for your dog to roam around in, but ideally you should provide a crate that he can call his own space.

The crate should be a positive place where your dog can relax. Therefore, the crate is never used for punishment. Do not use it for punishment, you will create a negative association to the crate and make your dog fear the crate. Instead he will search for a hiding place behind the furniture or otherwise in an unsafe place for his natural need for daily retreat.

Of course, the crate you choose needs to fit your dog. Buy a crate that will match your dog's grown size. When fully grown, he should be able to stand up, turn around, and lie down in this crate comfortably. The crate will seem too big when a puppy is little. In such a case simply block off the extra space at the back of the crate. You can use a box or hang a towel to do so. This will help to prevent in-crate-pooping too. Yes, I did just coin the phrase, in-crate-pooping. Use it free willingly. You have my blessings.

A crate that is enclosed with only slats for your dog to see out of on the sides and the front is ideal for dogs. He will want to observe his surroundings. This helps when things become noisy around him because he can see where the sounds come from.

The crate is not an isolation cell. However, you also want to make sure that the crate is not too open. It needs to be an enclosed den where he can have his privacy when needed. Open metal crates are not enclosed enough, cover it with a thick blanket, leaving narrow spaces on the sides that he can see out of.

Where to Place your Dog Crate
Place the crate close to where you spend the most time together while you are all awake in the house. Put it in a central area, against the wall. The idea is to keep your dog from feeling isolated and away from everything, while owning his own place in it too.

Furnishing the Crate
What you put in the crate is up to you. The crate should be a comfortable place where your dog can hang out as he wants, so be sure to place a pillow or some type

of dog bed in it. You can also put toys and treats in the crate.

It is a good idea to put clean water in the crate. To avoid spillage and a mess, get a water bowl that clips onto the crate's door. You can also attach a food bowl if you will be crating your dog for a lengthy period while you are away.

When your dog is left alone, he will miss you no matter how much training he gets, or from whom. A great trick to reduce anxiety is to leave a piece of your unwashed clothing inside with him, such as a sock or shirt. If you want it back in good condition, you will want to nip nipping and chewing in the bud first. Just saying.

5. Training Equipment

Before you start training your dog, you need to acquire the appropriate equipment. There are things that you absolutely need if you hope to train them properly and there are things that you do not need but make life easier. These things can train your dog to adopt certain behaviors.

Small Treats:

While training your dog you will be rewarding them with either treats or play. If you are using treats, then you need to get the right treats. The treats have to be small, easy to eat, and as healthy as possible.

During your training sessions with your dog you will be giving them a lot of treats, especially in the beginning. Every time your dog gets even a small portion of the behavior right you need to reward them in order to encourage them to continue. This is why the treats have to be healthy and small. If you are giving your dog a lot of treats and they are big and unhealthy then your dog will quickly suffer the consequences. They will become fat, unfit, and extremely unhealthy.

Your treats need to be small and easy to eat so it does not become a distraction during training. When you give your dog a treat, they need to be able to eat it straight away and get back to training. If the treat is too big or too chewy then the dog will spend longer eating it and they may lose focus in the training.

When you buy treats for your dog, look out for something they are going to like but make sure you get small, easy to eat, and healthy treats. If you find treats that are easy to eat and healthy but are too big for your dog, cut them up into small enough portions.

Clicker:

This is a common tool used by professional dog trainers. The tool makes a soft clicking noise and you can use it as an audio cue for your dog. When training you can reward them to let them know that they have done something right, but you can also use an audio cue. A simple word like "yes" or phrases such as "good girl" are commonly used but so is a clicker. When your dog does something, you want them to do, you use the clicker to signal they have done the right thing then reward them with a treat.

This is an optional buy, but it will make the training method easier. A clicker can also be used after the fact to make sure the behaviors you have taught your dog are not forgotten.

Whistle:

A whistle is commonly used when training your dog in public. A clicker is a soft and noticeable sound, but it only works indoors. When you are outside there are a lot of noises and distractions so a whistle works better to get your dog's attention.

A whistle is mostly used to teach your dog to come and also to teach them area denial. When there is an area in the park or outside where you do not want your dog to go, you simply blow the whistle whenever they get near it. This works if you have already taught the dog to come to you when they hear the whistle. After a while, the dog will not only associate the whistle with coming to you but also with those areas and they will know not to go there.

A whistle can be replaced by a few noise-making objects. If you have a metal leash for your dog, you can shake it and teach your dog to respond to the rattling metal. In most instances, the whistle is the best option.

Chew Toys and Puzzle Toys:

Dogs love to play so getting toys for them to play with is a must. You can get specific toys that can actually help your dog with their behavior training. Some toys are just meant to be fun, but others can train and mold your dog's behavior.

You can use chew toys to curve your dog's chewing habits. As mentioned before, one of the most annoying dog behaviors is their excessive chewing. You can use chew toys to train your dog to chew on them instead of the furniture.

Puzzle toys are toys that you can hide treats in. The challenge for your dog is to figure out how to get the treat out of the toy. This is good for developing their brain and their problem-solving skills. It is also useful for dogs with a lot of energy. They end up spending a lot of time getting the treat out of the toy and that gets rid of their excess energy. There are simple puzzle toys and complicated puzzle toys. Start with the simple ones and, when your dog can figure them out effortlessly, upgrade them to a more complicated puzzle.

Puzzle Food Bowl:

A puzzle food bowl is a normal food bowl but instead of just having all the food dumped in the middle it is made up of a hollow maze, so the food is spread out and not easy to get to. This is useful for several reasons.

1. Most dogs eat too fast and end up developing stomach problems. The puzzle food bowl forces them to eat slowly so they do not ruin their appetite or develop any stomach problems.

2. A puzzle food bowl helps the dog develop good problem-solving skills and good thinking skills.

3. A puzzle food bowl is an extremely useful tool for training a dog with food aggression. It forces them to eat slower and focus more on their food. This leaves

little room for them to focus on the things around them and therefore there is less opportunity for them to become aggressive. The slow eating time also means more training time.

That is all you really need to train your dog how to behave properly. There is other equipment you can get but these are the essentials. All of this will help your dog foster good habits from an early stage and they will help you with the training process.

Collar and Retractable Leash:

The right dog collar and a retractable leash will make training your dog outdoors easier. A retractable leash allows you to give your dog the exact amount of freedom that you think they deserve. This way you can see how your dog behaves away from you without the danger of letting them off the leash. The type of leash you get needs to fit your dog well. It cannot be too big, or it will slip off the moment your dog tries to get away from you. It cannot be too small, or it will be uncomfortable or even hurt your dog. It is a good idea to take your dog with you and try on several collars to see which one fits best.

A fully adjustable collar might be a good option if you have a small dog that is still growing. That way you will not have to buy another collar when they outgrow the one you just got them.

Some people prefer a normal leash to a retractable one. You can opt for a normal leash if that suits your training methods better. These are better for indoor training and really big dog breeds.

6. Methods of Housebreaking

Paper Training

The paper-training method is where you use newspapers and encourage your puppy to use these for going to the bathroom. You can also use special 'wee' pads that are scented with a chemical that attracts the puppy to use them. You can get these at any local pet store. They can make training easier, but they can be more costly as well. If you intend to continue using the pads, make sure you start with them and not paper. Do not mix newspaper and pads or your results will be very inconsistent.

The first thing you want to do is choose a confinement area, either in a very small room or a room that you can enclose with baby gates. Most people choose a bathroom, laundry room or kitchen area because these rooms are usually covered in tile or other flooring that is easy to keep clean. The confinement area should only be big enough for your pup's bed, food and water bowls, and his designated potty area.

There should be no visible floor space in the confinement area. The floor should have the bed or crate in one area, and newspapers or pads should cover the rest of the space. By using a small area, you are encouraging your pup to use the covered area of the floor to relieve himself. This will get him used to doing his business on the newspapers or pads. He will not potty in his bed or where he eats for reasons we have already tackled and since it is the only other space available, the potty area becomes a natural choice. The instincts that Mother Nature gave him will guide him away from his 'den' area to eliminate.

When he does soil on the newspapers, try to clean them up as quickly as possible. You may want to consider leaving a rag that has a little of his urine on it in the designated spot to help him recognize where he is supposed to go, if you're using newspaper. The pads are already scented to attract the puppy to go there. There are also house-training sprays you can buy at any big pet store that serve the same purpose. The pheromones in them attract puppy back to the right spot. These sprays can also be used outdoors if you want to direct him to a certain area.

Once your pup becomes accustomed to pottying on the newspapers, you can make the covered area smaller.

You should have noticed which part of the area he has used most often and keep all that part well covered. Start uncovering the area very close to his crate/bed and bowls. The goal is to continuously limit the designated 'inside potty area' by making the papered area smaller and smaller at the same time giving him frequent access to his 'outdoor potty area'. Therefore, it is important that you spend as much time as possible with your puppy so you can get him to his outdoor area as often as possible.

The key to quick and successful housebreaking when using the paper-training method really depends on how much supervised training you spend with your pup. The more times you can get him outside to do his business and reward him, the quicker he will learn.

Litter Pan Training

You have chosen a training area; now choose your dog's litter area. Choose an area that:

Will always be available to your puppy when he needs to eliminate.

Has a surface, such as gravel or concrete that is unlike any surface anywhere in your house. This ensures the puppy understands he is never to eliminate in the house.

In the early days of training, it is important for you to be with the dog each time he goes to the toilet area until he develops the habit of eliminating there. Your presence will help ensure he only uses the area you have established as his toilet area.

To make training easier and more predictable, settle on a feeding schedule, and stick to it. That way, his elimination habits will also be regular. If you can predict when your dog will need to eliminate, you can make sure you are available to accompany him, and guide him in using the area you've chosen – and nowhere else.

Your first goal is to get the dog to use the litter area regularly and to take him there, in case he needs to eliminate, several times a day. Once that routine is established, never confine the dog to his training area without giving him access to his toilet area. If he is unable to wait to eliminate and eliminates in his training area, it can set your house training back.

Crazy Training Pan

If you would like to streamline the housebreaking process, and you can completely free yourself from any other responsibilities, work or family, for a couple of days, then this 'extreme' method might be just the thing for you. It is very effective and creates a strong bond, but it does take its toll on you. If you are not a little bit crazy and open to things that are 'outside the box,' skip to the following part now. If, like me, you are a bit of a risk-taker, read on.

The 'crazy' way to house-train your pup, within his physical bladder limits of course, is to be completely proactive. The pup never goes on the floor, not once. How do you achieve this miracle, you ask? With self-sacrifice and a total focus on the task, allowing no distractions. It is just you, puppy, and housebreaking. This will work with a litter pan or a pad as well as going outdoors. It is actually a simple procedure, a sort of 'extreme crate training,' but you have to 'suck it up' and follow through—that's the craziness. It is 24/7 on your part until you reach his physical limits. After that, you never ask him to exceed those limits.

Still with me? Then here is how it goes. You bring puppy home and let him potty before you bring him inside. After Ten minutes, you take him out again (or take him to the pan or pad). Praise a successful trip! If he does not go, give him another ten minutes and then out again. After each successful potty break, you add five minutes to the time between trips, so you would wait 15 minutes and then go out again. After each unsuccessful trip, repeat the same interval. You need to continue this all day and all night, following and adjusting the schedule. Wake up (use an alarm), wake him up (really), and go out. (I slept on the sofa by the door to facilitate the process, while puppy slept tethered on the floor right to me.) Work some playtime in between some of the trips, and do not forget to wedge in some food for both you and the pup. Watch some TV together. But keep track of the time! You will become a little zombie-like, but that is OK. Think of it as a short-term extreme sporting event. Stay focused on your mission!

A three-month-old pup will settle into a 3-4-hour maximum interval between trips. Once you know what that limit is for your pup, you can make arrangements to let him relieve himself within that interval. You can also crate him and crawl into bed until your puppy potty break (set the alarm!).

Although you will need about a day to fully recover, depending on what time of day you brought him home and started the process, you will also have a very accurate idea of his bathroom habits and needs. You will have learned his potty rituals—does he sniff or circle, or both? (This can help you prevent future 'accidents' if he needs to go earlier than usual for some reason.) You have earned his trust, and he can count on you to meet, even anticipate, his needs. He is never eliminated anywhere except where you, his pack leader, have approved, so he will not be inclined to start. Even young as he is, he will come to you for a potty break. And, in spite of the sleep disruption, it is time spent working together that can give you a very strong bond with your dog. Packs work cooperatively for the good of all, and that is what you two have just done together!

The follow-up is simply assuring that you never expect him, or force him, to exceed his capabilities. You get him to his designated area within his time limit, period. If you cannot be there to do it, then you find someone who can help you out. This means at night, too! Set the alarm, take him for his potty break, praise, and go back to bed. Once he is 6 months old or so and has full control of himself, he will be extremely reliable (and sleeping through the night).

Crate Training Pan

Dogs need their own safe place to call home and relax. An owner's house might be a place to roam, but it is not the den that dogs crave. The crate satisfies a dog's longing for a den, and along with its many other uses provides comfort to them. All puppies should be taught to enjoy residing in their crate and know that it is a safe haven for them, so it is important never to use it for punishment. My friends Shih Tzu spend much of their sleeping time inside their crate where they feel safe and relaxed hidden away from a bustling home.

Before you begin crate, training give your dog a couple of days to adjust to his new home and surroundings. Crate training can be trained for a dog of any age. A dog's love for their crate is healthy and assists you in taking care of him or her throughout their lifetime.

Try to limit your puppy's time in the crate to around one hour per session. Never leave your adult dog in a crate for longer than five hours without providing them time outside of the crate. As your puppy matures and has learned proper dog etiquette (not chewing everything in sight), is housetrained, and can be trusted to run freely around your house, you can then leave the door open so that they can use it for their private bungalow to come and go as they choose.

I have listed below the benefits of crate, things to avoid, types, furnishings, the steps to crate train your dog, and troubleshooting, Godspeed.

Benefits of the Crate

It aids in housetraining because dogs are reluctant to soil their own sleeping area.

Acts as a mobile doghouse for trips via car, airplane, train, and then to be used at those destinations such as motels, and foreign houses.

The mobility can be utilized inside your own home by being moved throughout the house. *Especially beneficial during housetraining when you want your puppy near you:

- Can reduce separation anxiety.

- Keep your dog out of harm's way.
- Assists in chew-toy addiction.
- Aids your puppy in calming and quieting down.

Until he or she has learned that chewing, tearing, ripping of household and human items is forbidden, the crate keeps your dog shortly separated from destruction of those items.

7. Housebreaking Do's and Don'ts

Set aside the time needed to work with your puppy to establish proper toilet habits. The work you do with him now will ensure he is an enjoyable companion for years to come – or, if your training is spotty or rushed, it will ensure he is not. Give this training what it needs to be thorough and successful.

It is best to wait until your puppy is six months old to train him. Younger puppies are not able to control their bowel and bladder; to attempt training is to risk them feeling confused, shamed and in all ways negative around house training, and you do not want that.

Until your puppy is six months old, confine him to a room that's small and easily puppy proofed. Cover the floor with newspaper or some other absorbent material and be sure you change the paper every time it gets soiled. In the beginning, this can be a pretty demanding process, but as the puppy grows and uses a toilet area, you'll use less and less paper.

The Do's of House Breaking Your Puppy

- Your puppy should always be able to access his toilet area. To get him in the habit of using it when your home with him, take him to his toilet area at least every 45 minutes.

- If you cannot be home or are busy with something and cannot supervise your dog, put him in his puppy-proofed room lined with paper and free of anything he might chew on or eat. That way, he will not soil his training area.

- The puppy's toilet area should be a surface that is unlike any floor in your home. Possibilities are concrete, asphalt, grass or dirt. Do not choose a toilet area surface that in any way resembles hardwood floors, carpet or tile.

- You should praise your puppy and reward him when he uses the toilet area to eliminate. Your puppy needs to associate using the toilet area with things that are positive and that make him happy – toys, treats and lots of enthusiastic praise.

- Keep your puppy on a feeding schedule, and give him plenty of clean, fresh water to drink. That way, you can better predict when he will need to go to his toilet area, and you can plan to accompany him.

- Consider using a crate for housetraining your puppy. Information on how to crate train follows in this part.

- Above all, remember to be patient throughout the process of housetraining your dog. Give it all the time it takes – and it could take several months. That may seem like a long time, but you are training your dog to be a companion to you and your family for years to come. Best to train him right the first time.

The Don'ts of House Training Your Puppy:

- Never lose your patience or your temper with your puppy over mistakes. Remember – punishing him will just confuse him and cause him to be fearful. It will set your training back.

- Do not leave food out for your puppy to eat all day or all night. Establish a feeding schedule and pick up any uneaten food. That way you can better predict your puppy's toilet schedule.

- Go from training area to one additional room, and then another, and take your time. Do not let your puppy have free access to the rest of the house until you have thoroughly trained him.

8. Putting Your Dog on a Schedule

Why it is It Important to Keep My Dog on a Daily Schedule?

The most important thing to do for your dog is to create a routine for it. Dogs need to be able to stick to a schedule. It gives them assurance that they will be safe and protected.

Make sure that you are feeding at the same time every day. If they have a random feeding schedule, it will be stressful for them because they will never really know whether or not they will have food to eat. They will also worry that they will not be able to eat when they are hungry.

They will go to the bathroom around the same time as well. It should be a routine for them to wake up and go outside, go before bed, and a few similar timeframes throughout the day.

Sleep is essential for them. Some dogs can get anxious and not be able to fully sleep. If they do not have a schedule, they might not be able to become relaxed enough to get that deep sleep needed.

Most importantly, have an exercise routine. Not only will it be good for your pup, but you will benefit from these periods of high activity as well. They will know the difference between play time and relax if you make sure that you are carving out specific times for them to exercise. Rather than having an active pup that acts all wild, you can have a dog that knows when it is time to lay down and when it is time to be crazy and play.

Make sure that you are also conscious of the methods that they might be associating place and specific locations with parts of their routine. For example, ensure that they have a proper place to sleep every night and that it is consistent. They will know when you take them to this place, that it is time to sleep. Have them eat in a similar place as well. If they are led to their food bowl, they will know that it is time to eat.

Not every day is going to have the same schedule, but when you are doing those routine things, they should have the same structure each time. Keep procedures consistent so that there is no confusion on your dog's end.

Taking them to the bathroom first thing in the morning is a good habit. At the same time, it is ok to wait just a few minutes if you need to set up the coffee or go to the bathroom first yourself. You do not want to rush and stress your dog out with that first morning bathroom trip. Give yourself enough time so that this period can be calm and relaxing for your dog.

15 minutes a day is the minimum playtime you should have for ALL dogs. The bigger the dog, the more exercise they will need. If they have a day where they do not get out much, make sure that they are twice as active the following day.

A Sample Puppy Schedule

Time	Activity
6:30 a.m.	Puppy exercise: Walk the dog around the street/park.
7:00 a.m.	Early Morning meal
8:00 a.m.	Play time
10:00 a.m.	Nap time
Noon	Lunch time
1:00 p.m.	Nap time
3:00 p.m.	Playtime
5:00 p.m.	Evening meal
7:00 p.m.	Playtime
9:00 pm	Bedtime

9. Potty Training Process

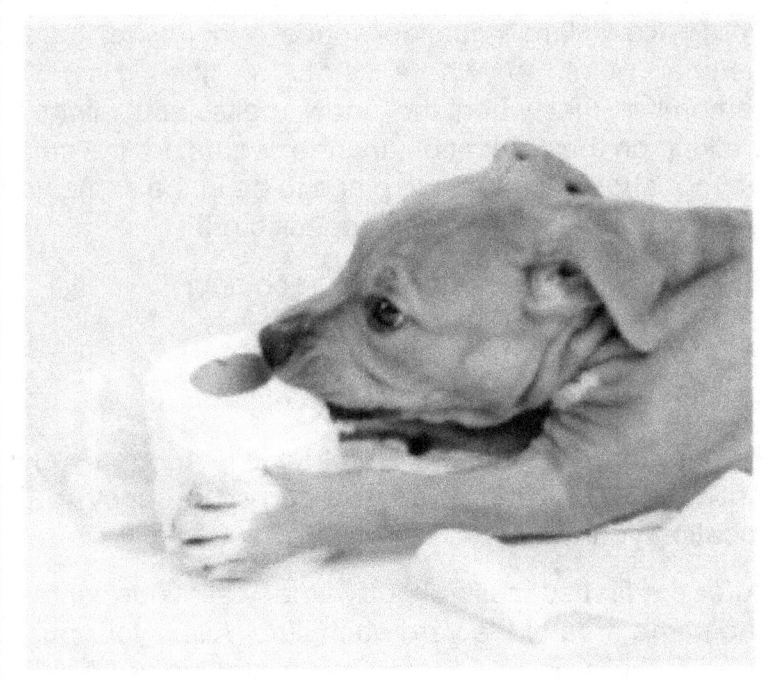

The fact states, your puppy for every month of life can hold their bladder an hour each. A puppy who is just four weeks, needs to be let outside nearly every hour. As the owner and the human, it is your responsibility to ensure your puppy is let outside or housetrained. You cannot get angry at your puppy because he/she pees or poops in the wrong location, or any inside location, if you make him/her hold their needs.

It would be like asking a newly potty-trained child to hold it because you do not want to go into a bathroom right now.

Choose the Rules

It is also your responsibility to choose the rules of where your puppy is allowed to pee and defecate. If you have a large outside space and do not care if he/she goes anywhere that is fine. However, remember that when the snow melts, you might be walking on the defecation. In other words, for the safety of your shoes, if you have plans to be in the same yard area, you may want to set a specific rule.

Start by taking your puppy out each hour.

Go with your puppy.

Call his/her name and have him follow you.

If your puppy tries to pee or defecate in an area you do not want, pick him/her up and carry the puppy to the location you want.

After the first successful potty time, walk your puppy to the same area of the yard each time. Allow your puppy to sniff the area and remember this is his/her allowed location.

You may not care where in the yard your puppy goes, but you want it to be the same each time. For this, you can let your puppy pick a spot. After that spot is picked, then you can bring your puppy to that location each time he/she needs to go. Always pick him/her up if the puppy does not return to the same spot.

Let your puppy sniff the old spot.

If your puppy has learned commands, it will be easier; however, most will need to be taught outside toileting rules before they are old enough to learn the voice commands.

Never yell.

Never say "no."

Just be calm, pick up your puppy and place them on the spot they should go. If the matter is urgent, your puppy will immediately be set down and go to the bathroom.

Repetition will ensure follow through.

What to do if your Puppy is not listening

There is a chance that your puppy will not come when called, will not sit or stay, and follow the rule of going to the bathroom in a specific location.

It means you need to provide more training with a reward they want.

Your puppy likes praise, treats, and feeling comfortable.

You may need to start off with treats; particularly, if there is an issue with listening.

Take your puppy to the right location.

Let him/her sniff around.

If she/he goes to the bathroom, provide a treat.

Other time take your puppy to the right spot.

If he/she tries to go elsewhere and succeeds before you can stop him/her, do not provide a treat.

Only when the right location is used, will you provide a treat.

You always want to reward good behavior, ignore the bad, and certainly never yell.

It might take several tries, but after your puppy learns there is something good waiting with the right toileting spot, the puppy will be more inclined to listen.

10. Top Training Techniques

Train Your Dog to Use His Paws

The trick of a dog contribution you its paw is a basic yet exceptionally engaging one. It will not take long for you to training your dog to give you his paw, however it should just be educated in short blasts, over a couple of days.

In the long run your dog will have the option to give you its paw and afterward even shake paw-to-hand with you.

Most dogs will do about anything to satisfy their owners. Dogs are commonly anxious to get applause and fondness, which is the reason training done right can create the ideal outcomes in brief period.

For instance, you can train your dog to shake rapidly and effectively, basically by knowing the means. Despite the fact that this specific direction isn't one for compliance, it is adorable and fun.

A few people will show their dog to shake while others favor a progressively hip direction of "Give me five, Paw, "Put it there", and so forth.

Notwithstanding, relatives and companions will be intrigued at the trick your dog can perform. At that point, when he has aced the shake direction, you could proceed onward to other and even propelled tricks.

Right now, needed to give you instances of how you can train your dog to shake, rapidly and effectively.

- Start by picking the direction word or expression that will be utilized and afterward be steady, as not to befuddle your dog
- you can train your dog to shake using the left or right paw or both
- Make sure you have a couple of little, yet sound treats in your pocket, which will be utilized as a prize, alongside verbal commendation and petting
- Tapping your dog's paw from the underneath, urge him to lift his paw while giving him the picked direction
- Hold his paw for around five seconds, trailed by a treat and applause

- Repeat the lifting and holding steps, holding up a couple of moments longer before lifting the paw and afterward consistently give a prize commendation when the paw is in your grasp
- With training, your dog will before long comprehend that when you state the order word, he is to lift the paw with or without a treat albeit uplifting feedback as recognition and petting ought to be given unfailingly
- To train your dog to shake, experience five instructional courses each day until he at long last gets it
- If keen on showing your dog to shake with the other paw or the two paws, essentially experience the procedure utilizing the ideal paw or by rotating with the two paws for every session.

After the "sit" command, the shake trick is one of the most effortless for a dog to learn.

Normally, you can have your dog shaking in about a week or less. Truth be told, with somewhat more time and exertion, you can show your dog to play out the trick essentially by highlighting the paw.

How to show your puppy to Wave?

After of acing 'Shake Hands' 'Shake' command, you can instruct how to 'Wave' to your puppy. Ask your dog 'shake hands' direction to your dog, reach down to take his paw yet do not contact the paw.

Haul your hand back simply out of paw reach and state "great Wave" his paw is noticeable all around hanging tight for you to take it.

The majority of the dogs attempt to arrive at your hand and put their paw noticeable all around.

Be cautious with this direction in light of the fact that your puppy will be confounded on the grounds that you give the order and you didn't take the paw you should.

Commendation your dog merrily while your dog's paw is noticeable all around, so they realize this is the correct move for the direction.

After of rehearsing 20 - multiple times your dog will comprehend when you state 'shake hands wave' you will not take the paw.

Quit saying 'Shake hands' and simply request that your dog 'wave' presently. If the person just lifts paw, however, does not wave so you may should be increasingly energized, give the directions in progressively lively mode.

Begin instructional meeting from the earliest starting point.

Reach for the paw of your dog to urge him to stretch out his paw to you and move it. Make sure to keep these instructional meetings short.

The High Five

This trick expands upon the last one of showing your dog to give you the paw. If you have not trained your dog to give you the paw, at that point it is ideal to instruct that trick before endeavoring this one.

By and by have a few treats good to go. Grasp a treat and afterward lift your hand somewhat higher than you did in the past trick. The purpose behind this is to get your dog to believe that you are doing the paw trick, the dog will at that point raise his paw towards yours.

When your dog does this, say the order 'High Five' at that point reward the person in question with the treat. In the event that you have the paw trick aced with your dog, at that point you will locate this one simple and it won't take long for your dog to learn.

How to Train Your Dog to Jump

In the event that your dog has aced fundamental directions, for example, heel, sit and remain, hop would be a decent order to instruct straightaway. By following the means recorded beneath, you can train your dog to hop.

You will require at any rate one sort of hop to start, for example, the bar. You might need to have a few kinds to mix it up. Set the bars to the most minimal level with the goal that all the dog needs to do is stroll across it.

To start, put a rope on your dog, and hold the chain with two hands. Approach the hop, give the hop order, and lead your pet over the obstacle. When he arrives at the opposite side of the obstacle, give the heel direction.

Be liberal with your recognition. As your pet experts the obstacle at the most reduced level, continue raising the level a score at resulting instructional courses.

The way to teaching the hop order is to never let the creature will not bounce. If your dog recoils, continue bringing down the bounce until he at last goes over it.

Something else, your pet may decline to hop all the time since the person in question has gotten by with rejecting previously.

When your pet has gotten familiar with the obstacles and will go over them when you give the order, you are trained to let the dog play out the activity all alone with you holding the lead.

As he bounces, make certain to hold the rope straight before the focal point of the obstacle and afterward bring your arm down as the person lands. Give bunches of recognition.

When your dog can heel and bounce without you giving remedies, you are presently trained to let the dog play out the activity off lead. Approach the obstacle, point to it, and issue the direction to hop. Rapidly stroll by the obstacle and afterward walk gradually while giving the heel direction and tapping your side.

Be certain not to run when moving toward the obstacle, since this energizes dogs and makes them less inclined to help out you. Likewise, continue training fun and recognition your pet eagerly. If you feel yourself getting disappointed, stop and accomplish something your pet appreciates, for example, a round of bring so you will not distance him from working with you.

You can utilize the means above to training your dog to bounce on direction. The majority of all, appreciate investing the one-on-one energy with your pet.

The first and most significant thing to recall when training a dog is teaching feedback. Continuously reward your dog's acceptable conduct (with a clicker, treat or a decent stroke) as opposed to rebuffing negative conduct. Remember, dogs need to please; it is a piece of their hereditary cosmetics, so utilize this reality to further your potential benefit.

It is shrewd to start training your dog from as young as could be allowed. Consequently, in the event that you have another puppy in the house, don't ruin him, or her, spoiled for the primary month and afterward stress over the dog's noncompliance.

It is in no way, shape or form difficult to training a dog of all ages, yet all together for your dog to remember you as the pack chief, you should act like it from the very first moment.

Along these lines, your home guidelines, for example, no eating from the table or no sitting on the furnishings, ought to be actualized from the earliest starting point.

3 Manners That Your Dog Should Have

No begging: the most ideal approach to dishearten asking is to guarantee that nobody in the family sneaks' nourishment under the table.

There are numerous human nourishments that ought not be given to dogs, however, if you have a bit of remaining meat (or something comparable), make your dog hold up until everybody has completed the feast before offering it to him, or her.

No jumping: If your dog is the neighborly sort, he, or she, will bounce on outsiders in the event that you permit him, or her, to hop on you.

Besides, setting the front paws on your shoulders can be a sign of testing your power, so despite the fact that you may think that its tender and worthy, it ought to be disheartened.

Try not to be possessive over toys: For cases when your dog has gotten something it should not or a thing that represents a risk, it is significant that you can remove any object from him, or her. Start by irregularly removing most loved toys from your dog while it is as yet young.

This may appear to be unfeeling, yet it just should be for a couple of moments.

If he, or she, does not respond forcefully to you taking the toy or bone, (which will very likely be the situation) offer bunches of recognition and return the thing.

Assuming, nonetheless, there is some snarling or other indication of aggression, it is critical to do the activity all the more much of the time and keep the thing for longer timeframes. You dog should view all toys and bones as yours - you just permit him, or her, to play with them.

Obviously, these are only a bunch of things that you ought to consider when training your dog. If you are experiencing difficulty with training, look for the counsel of an expert compliance mentor or a veterinarian.

11. Cures for Behavior Issues in Dogs

Demands your attention

If a dog starts to bother you, then he wants something, usually because this action proves rewarding. If your dog barks at you, and you give him what he wants, he is going to start barking because it worked. If he is nosing you, and you are petting him, he is going to start nosing you. If he drops the ball in your lap and noses your hand before you throw it, and you do, he is going to keep giving you the ball. When he paws at you to get you to do something, and you do it, he is going to keep pawing at you.

One thing that can make their attention-demanding worse is being unnecessarily mad at your dog, showering him with excessive affection, and allowing him to sleep with you in your bed. Some dogs will sleep in your bed just fine, with no side effects. Others can become excessively reliant. This is not a good connection to your dog, and it can lead to stress when separated and produce an anxious, depressed dog.

You should love your dog and take care of him without spoiling him rotten. If your dog shows signs of attention-demand or an inability to leave you alone, you need to fix it before it gets worse.

The dog will never stop wanting your attention until you stop giving it to him. It is going to be challenging at first. Both of you are going to change your habits. Behavior usually increases until it is extinguished–it is a normal thing. This means that if your dog barks for attention, and you have been giving it to him for a while now, his barking may get worse when you suddenly stop. You have got to wait him out. When you give in, it is going to be that much harder for him to break his habit. Another important idea is to focus on your preparation. Through daily training sessions, your dog can learn to get your attention by performing behaviors for you.

Barking

Barking dogs will drive you nuts. They can ruin ties with neighbors and make you feel humiliated in public. There are several explanations as to why dogs bark:

- Certain breeds of dogs, such as those in the herding community, are natural barkers, and there may be a strong genetic component to the issue.

- It may be satisfying. For example, if your dog barks at you and you pay attention to him, he is going to increase the action because it worked.

- They are alerting you of something. Alarm barking happens when a dog senses something and wants to report it. This can involve a cat outside the window or someone entering the house.

- Fear.
- Wanting you or another animal to play.
- Frustration.
- Predation or the search of something.
- Restlessness.
- A greeting.

The first thing you need to do to avoid the barking is to decide why your dog does it, if you can. That means you can treat or ignore it, that often solves the problem. For example, if your dog barks only at the window, just block your dog's access to the window.

You are trying to prevent your dog from exhibiting actions. It can become an ingrained habit if he keeps it up. Unless the problem is not fear-related, and your dog is simply barking because he is excited about it, you should teach your dog to stick to the hint.

Goal: Your dog is going to be quiet when you say the hint.

What you are going to need:

- Clicker
- Treats

1. Find something to make the dog bark. Wait for him to quit on his own.

2. The second he stops, click and treat.

3. Repeat steps 1-2 at least 9 times. End the training session.

If your dog interrupts his barking really easily, it's time to add the hint.

1. Find something to make the dog bark.

2. Right before you think he's going to be silent, say "hush" or "silent, be consistent. Use your hint once, in a polite voice. When you scream at your dog, he is probably only going to bark louder, assuming you are going to join in!

3. Click and treat when your dog is quiet.

4. Repeat steps 1-3 at least 9 times. End the training session.

Begging

Dogs beg for food for a variety of reasons. When you ever feed your dog from the bed, he will know that it is fun to hang out to you while you are eating. He may start asking you for more food. Dogs will also understand that the eating area itself is tempting if crumbs are on the surface.

Teach your dog to 'settle' so that he can learn to go to a mat or bed while you are eating. Once he is on his mat, give him a toy that is stuffed with food so he can enjoy a treat while you are eating, too.

Car Anxiety/Carsickness

Dogs can get motion sick just like us humans do. You do not want to make a car ride uncomfortable for your dog. Speak to your doctor about treats' that can help to relieve your dog's symptoms. You can teach your dog to enjoy car rides more, but you can use medicine to help with the process if necessary.

Goal: Your dog is going to enjoy car rides.

What you are going to need:

- Clicker
- Treats.

Start this move if your dog is becoming anxious when approaching a vehicle.

1. When your dog shows some interest in the vehicle, or just looks at the vehicle, click and treat him.

2. Take a slight step closer to your vehicle. Click and treat when your dog looks at the vehicle or if he runs towards it.

3. Repeat step 2 a few times but quit if your dog is showing signs of anxiety. The stage at which he has stress can differ, depending on your dog, so pay attention to his signals. For future training sessions, build up to where you can get your dog in the car and lock it in your crate or seat belt, so it is not stressed out.

When your dog is ready to get into the car, keep training with the following moves. If you are trying to drive, you are not going to be able to use treats safely. Plus, since nausea is always a factor, you do not want to feed your dog and make the nausea worse.

1. Start your car while your dog is in it. Let it run for 2 seconds as you praise your dog for being in it. Switch the engine off and take your dog out of the vehicle. Getting out of the car is going to be a treat for your dog.

2. Repeat step 1, slowly through the time you dog is in a moving vehicle. Move up to a couple of minutes. When your dog feels anxious, you are working too hard. Repeat no more than 5 times, or less if the dog is nervous.

3. Once your dog is comfy with step 2, place your dog in the car, start the engine, drive the car down the alley, drive back to the initial position of the car, turn the engine off and remove your dog. Praise your dog while the car is on the move. Do not do more than 5 times, or less if your dog is nervous.

4. Once your dog is relaxed with step 3, restart it, taking increasingly longer drives. You can go around the block the first time you leave your house. When you come back to your house, turn the car off and remove your dog from the vehicle. Repeat no more than 5 times, or less if the dog is nervous.

Tips: These brief driving sessions will slowly acclimate your dog to a car ride. The way you protect your dog in the car will help, too. Dogs should always be protected in vehicles; they should never be left loose to wander the vehicle. If your dog is afraid to ride in a car and is usually crated, consider a canine seatbelt. On the other hand, if your dog has a car phobia and is usually in a seatbelt, consider a crate. The adjustment may have an effect on making him feel better in the car.

Running or Herding

Running is highly rewarding for most dogs. Some breeds are genetically engineered to hunt. When your corgi is chasing the kids, it is just because his DNA is telling him to do it! But that does not mean you have to let your natural hunter go after things.

Teach your dog 'leave it'. With proper understanding of 'leave it', it is going to help teach your dog that not running after something can be just as rewarding. Also, introduce your dog to the fun of chasing a long pole toy instead of your kids.

Counter-Surfing

When you have a very tall dog that can reach the counter, it will start exploring them sooner. Such explorations are also rewarding. The first time the dog lands a ham sandwich, he learns that the counter is a treasure chest.

Management is the first step in the prevention of counter-surfing. Block your dog's access to the counter unless you are there to track his actions. Otherwise, you are just giving him a chance to exercise his new conduct. Keep your counters free of anything he could find tempting. Train 'leave it' and use it when you see him standing up and placing his paws on the counter. If you want to do it unattended in the kitchen, leave a few food-stuffed chew toys on the floor. The objective is to guide your dog's attention to the floor rather than the counter.

Digging

Just like some dogs are born to hunt, others are born to dig. Terriers, for instance, were originally bred to track and hunt vermin. Digging is a good characteristic for an animal that has been bred to go after mice and voles. Dogs dig because it is fun. Often it can be hard to believe that 2 tiny front paws will dig such deep holes! Yet, it is a habit that many people find irritating and harmful. To stop your dog from digging, you need to track him to deter and redirect his actions. If you do not, you cannot tell him not to dig.

That means you are going to have to treat the situation. Do not lock your dog out when you are away from home, rather, bring him into your house. You can also train him if you are worried, he is going to have accidents or he is going to be aggressive if he's left alone indoors. When you are out, guide your dog to activities that you like better than digging. Give him toys, and sometimes rotate toys so that he does not get bored with them.

12. Giving Dog Treats

Here are some treat thoughts:

- Whole grain oats are acceptable, for example, cheerios without sugar included are a decent decision.

- Kibble (dry nourishments). Put some in a paper pack and lift the fragrance factor by hurling in some bacon or another meat item. Canines are about those yummy smell sensations.

- Beef Jerky that has no pepper or overwhelming flavoring included.

- Carrots, apple pieces, and a few mutts even appreciate melons.

- Meats that have been cubed and are not profoundly prepared or salted, these are anything but difficult to make at home also. You can utilize cooked left-over nourishments.

- Shredded cheddar, string cheddar or cubed cheddar. Mutts love cheddar!

- Cream cheddar, nutty spread, or splash cheddar. Give your canine a little dab to lick for each legitimate conduct. These function admirably when preparing pups to ring a bell to go outside for end.

- Baby food meat items, they surely do not look yummy to us, however hounds revere them.

- Ice Cubes, however on the off chance that your pooch has dental issues, continue circumspectly.

- Commercial canine treats, however, use alert, there are heaps of them available. Search for those that do not have additives, results, or counterfeit hues. Furthermore, think about the nation of root.

Never feed or treat your four-legged companion from the eating table, since you would prefer not to encourage that asking activities are worthy. While treating, give treats a long way from the supper table or from zones that individuals regularly accumulate to eat, for example, by the BBQ.

Time to Treat

The best time to give hound treats is between suppers. Getting excessively close dinner times makes all treats less viable, so recollect this when arranging your instructional meetings. In the event that during preparing you have to pull together your pooch once more into the instructional course, keep a high worth treat for possible afterward use.

Clearly, if your pooch is full of supper time, he will be less inclined to need a treat prize than if somewhat ravenous. In the event that your canine isn't ravenous, your instructional courses will probably be progressively troublesome and far less viable. This is the reason it is a smart thought to remunerate right activities with applause, play, or toys, and not to depend only on treats.

- Love and consideration are viewed as remunerations and is absolutely uplifting feedback that can be similarly as powerful as an eatable treat. Pooch treating is contained edibles, acclaim, and consideration. Taking part in play or permitting some quality time with their preferred rope toy is additionally successful and on occasion, these prizes are pivotal to hound preparing.

- Do not give your canine a treat without requesting an activity first. State "sit" and after your pooch consents convey the treat. This strengthens your preparation and their dutifulness.

- Avoid treating your canine when he is over animated and running amuck in an unfocused perspective. This can be counterproductive and might fortify a negative conduct bringing about the powerlessness to stand out enough to be noticed.

- Due to their sharp feeling of smell, they will know well before you would ever realize that there is a scrumptious nibble close by yet keep it far out. Issue your order and trust that your pooch will obey before introducing the prize. Recall when canine treating, it is essential to be understanding and cherishing, however it is similarly significant not to give the treat until your pooch complies.

- Some mutts have a characteristic delicacy to them and consistently take from your hand tenderly, while different pooches need some direction to accomplish this. On the off chance that your pooch is somewhat unpleasant during treat getting, feel free to prepare the order "delicate!" when giving treats. Be firm starting now and into the foreseeable future. Give no treats except if they are delicately taken from your hand. Stay relentless with your choice to execute this, and soon your little guy will agree in the event that he needs the delectable treat.

13. One Week Formula of Housebreaking

DAY 1
What to Know Before Training

Celebrating is not the only point you need to understand before you start training. You need to understand that your dog's personality depends on how well they will train. You need to know about training tools, how your dog's age matters, and how your mindset matters.

Put Thought into the Name

Naturally, you will choose a name that you love, but if you know you'll spend a lot of time training your new family member, it's important to think of a name that will catch your dog's attention. Names with strong consonants that are short work great. They will perk up your dog's ears, making it easier for you to catch their attention. Some great names to consider are Ginger, Jack, and Jasper.

You may think you can only give your little eight-week-old puppy a name and not your older dog you received from the shelter. It's important to know the name of your dog from the shelter tends to be temporary. While this isn't always the case, most shelters don't know the dog's name when they receive them. Call your dog by their shelter name and notice their reaction. If they don't respond, they don't know that you are calling them, and you can rename your dog. Even if you have a dog that responds to a name, you can still change it. This can give you a good start on learning how to train your dog.

Have One Consistent Way to Grab Your Dog's Attention

Dogs are easily distracted by their environment, especially puppies. This causes problems with training because their owners feel they aren't listening to them. In reality, your dog became distracted and didn't know you were talking to them. By setting up a way to grab your dog's attention, such as calling their name, you will train them to look at you.

For example, you notice your dog is in the yard sniffing something on the ground, but they are too close to the road. Because the way you get your dog's attention is to snap your fingers, you head outside and snap your fingers twice. Even though you are several feet from your dog, they are used to this sound and know you are calling to them. They look up and listen to your command to "come."

DAY 2

Once your puppy is leash trained, walking him is an enjoyable way for the two of you to bond and provides you with time to clear your mind and get some exercise, too.

The Normal Puppy

An untrained puppy isn't aware of the dangers around him. He will strain against his leash, and he'll hate that he can't get free. He'll buck, jump, and do anything he can to get out of his harness or collar. He'll also want to stop and smell everything he can. A puppy gets a lot of information from his sense of smell, and he can tell if something is good or bad, if another animal has been around, or even if it's just interesting to him.

Introduce the Collar

There are dozens of different collar and leash styles to choose from, and the best one for you will depend on your dog. Small dogs do well in a harness so they can't slip out of their collars. That works well for puppies of all breeds.

When you first introduce the collar to your pup, be sure it fits properly. There should be enough room for you to fit two fingers between the collar and your pup's neck. Make putting the collar on fun by using an upbeat, but calm voice and reward your pup with a treat once the collar is fastened. Some puppies will try to push the collar off or scratch at it; after all, it is a new sensation.

DAY 3
Giving the Treat

Try to avoid treating your dog when he is over stimulated and running amuck and in an unfocused state of mind. This can be a counterproductive treating as it may reinforce a negative behavior or you may be unable to get your dog's attention.

When giving the treat allow your dog to get a big ole doggie whiff of that tasty food treat, but keep it up and away from a quick snatch and grab. Due to their keen sense of smell, they will know long before you figure it out that there is a tasty snack nearby. Issue your command and wait for him to obey before issuing the doggie reward. Remember when dog treating to be patient and loving, but do not give the treat until he obeys. Try to use the treating to reward the kickback mellow dog not the out of control or over-excited dog.

Some dogs have a natural gentleness to them and always take from your hand gently, other dogs need some guidance regarding taking the treat from your hand in a manner that is gentle. If your dog is a bit rough on the ole treat grabbing hand, go ahead and train the command "Gentle" when giving treats. Be firm that from this point forth no treats will be given unless taken gently. Being steadfast with this decision will work well and soon your pup or dog will comply if he wants his tasty treat.

Time to Treat

The best time to be issuing dog treats is in between his or her meals. If training always keep the tastiest treat in reserve in case you need to reel your dog's attention back to the training session. Too close to meal times all treats are less effective so keep that in mind when planning you training sessions. Obviously if your dog is full from mealtime he will be less likely to want a treat reward than if he is a bit hungry, therefore your training session is apt to be more difficult and far less effective.

DAY 4

This day is where we get to some of the fun stuff about training! We are going to look at some of the steps that you can take in order to teach your puppy some basic commands. There are a lot of different commands that you are able to teach your puppy, but we are going to focus on some of the basic ones that will make your life with your puppy a little bit easier. Some of the basic commands that we need to take a look at include:

- Sit
- Lay down
- Stay
- Wait
- Wait
- Come
- Shake
- Heel

DAY 5

You need to praise your puppy verbally when he relieves himself in the correct spot. When he makes a good decision, you need to praise him. If you do not do this, it will slow your progress down because he knows that there is nothing for him if he is not praised. When you give your puppy a treat after he goes in the right place, he knows that he will get something in return if he goes in the right spot. This will make him want to pee or poop only in that spot.

Expecting too Much

Your puppy is learning slowly, and he has had a few clean days. You may assume that he is now going to do everything right, but you need to understand that there is a lot more that you need to do. You cannot expect your puppy to understand everything about training until. You cannot slack off on the basics too soon because that will lead to accidents. You should continue to stick to the program until you are certain that your puppy understands.

DAY 6
Don't Push Aside the Crate

It's easy for you to see a crate as a jail cell for a dog, but dogs see a crate as a place to call their own. As long as you don't make your dog stay in the crate most of the day, you will find your dog lounging in their crate at times.

One factor to consider with a crate is how you will use it. If you want to use the crate as a way to punish your dog for bad behavior, you won't want them sleeping in the crate. In this case, you will want to think about getting a bed and a crate or two different types of crates. You don't want to tell your dog to go to bed in the same crate you give them a time out in because they can confuse the two meanings. If your dog feels you are angry with them during the night, they aren't going to sleep well, causing them to become sick or depressed.

Think About Your Training and Discipline

Some people use training as a way to combat disciplining their dog. They believe training their dog to listen to their commands and using a firm voice is all they need. For most dogs, this will work as long as you are training your dog correctly and consistently. Even if this is the way you want to go, it is helpful to look into the best ways to use any form of discipline. You also need to be aware that certain forms of discipline will have serious consequences.

Correctly disciplining your dog is not an easy task. It will take planning and ensuring that every family member is on the same page. This is something you will also need to do with training. To effectively discipline your dog, consider the following tips:

DAY 7
Consistency Is Key

One of the strongest ways to effectively train your dog is remaining consistent. It is always possible you won't catch your dog in action or be unable to reach your dog when they misbehave, meaning you have to let this one slide as they won't understand what they did wrong. When it comes to these moments, you need to realize they happen. The trick is to not let them happen often. Professional trainers say you have about five seconds to correct your dog's behavior. Once this time passes, you need to let it go and try to catch them in the act the next time.

Patience Is another Key

Another strong key feature when it comes to training is patience. If you have expectations that your dog will learn to sit by the end of the day, you must lower your expectations. It will take days to weeks to train your dog one trick and you will never stop training.

You will need more patience for a dog you just brought home as it takes them time to adjust to their new environment and for an older dog. Senior dogs are slower than puppies. They aren't going to catch on to new tricks as quickly and can show more stubbornness because they are used to their ways. However, with patience, consistency, and positive reinforcement you will teach your old dog new tricks.

14. Common Dog Training Mistakes

The Mistake: Not recognizing signs of fear and anxiety from your dog.

Years ago, we owned a self-service dog wash from a franchise. As one of our regular customers was drying his dog with the dryer, the dog was sitting on the grooming table, leaning against the wall, yawning repeatedly. Our customer said that was how he could tell his dog really liked his baths, because he was so relaxed during them, he would yawn and almost fall asleep.

Oh my. His dog was anything but relaxed. The reason the dog was leaning against the wall was because he was trying to get as far away from the dryer as possible.

He had pulled his ears back against his head, and his tail was tucked tight in a half circle against his legs. Both of these are body postures typical of fearful dogs.

Yawning in this context was not a sign of relaxation. Instead, it's what behaviorists call a displacement behavior. These are normal behaviors that are displaced out of their usual context. They are an indication the dog is uncertain and somewhat anxious about what to do. The dog is conflicted about doing one behavior versus another, so to resolve the conflict he does neither. Instead, he chooses a displacement behavior.

In Fido's case, the dog's choices were to jump down off the table (risking the displeasure of and a "correction" from his owner) or stay where he was. As he was trying to decide which was the lesser of two evils for him, he yawned to manage his conflict and anxiety.

Granted, that description is a bit anthropomorphic, but nevertheless the existence of displacement behaviors in conflict situations is well established. And like our customer, most dog owners either do not notice them, misinterpret their meaning, or are not aware such behaviors are extremely important in understanding their dog's behavior.

Recent research bears out our experiences with dog owners. Dr. Michele Wan, a Certified Applied Animal Behaviorist, and our friend and colleague, found that dog owners and professionals with less than 10 years of experience had more trouble identifying signs of fear, stress and anxiety from dogs than did professionals with over 10 years of experience.

Dr. Wan's research* further tells us that regardless of our experience with dogs, people are mostly able to identify when a dog is happy. It is identifying the fear, stress, and anxiety that trips people up. Because most bites occur from fearful dogs, missing these signs can have very bad consequences. At the very least, allowing stress, anxiety, and fear to go unrecognized in our dogs prevents us from either relieving or preventing these conditions, decreases their quality of life, and can even contribute to disease and a variety of behavior problems.

The Reasons People Make This Mistake

Displacement behaviors are a specialized group of behaviors that you would be unlikely to know about unless you had talked to a behavior professional or taken an animal behavior course. Much of the information about canine communication signals that is more easily accessible to the general public in the popular media is either incomplete or just plain wrong.

For example, most people have been taught that a wagging tail that indicates a dog is friendly. While a tail that is furiously wagging in a wide sweeping motion is probably a sign of friendliness, a more measured stiff-looking side-to-side wag is part of an offensive threat. But the popular media usually does not tell you that.

Second, there is a real difference between casually watching your dog versus carefully observing his body postures and how they change from moment to moment. And there is also a difference between observing behaviors and interpreting them. You likely have a lot of experience watching your dog's behaviors.

Nobody spends more time with your dog than you do. You are best able to notice when her behavior changes because you know what is normal and typical for her. But you may not always know what features of your dog's body language are more important, or how to interpret what you see.

I'll spend the rest of this part improving your observational skills and tell you the different features of your dog's body to pay attention to, so you will better know when your dog is scared, anxious or stressed.

The Mistake: Failing to reinforce good behavior.

When you receive good service from a company, how often do you take the time to write a letter thanking the service provider and commending the company on a job well done? Unless you had an extraordinary experience, my prediction is you have written very few of these letters. I know I have not, I am ashamed to admit. It is uncommon for any of us to go out of our way, other than perhaps to say 'thank-you', to reward good behavior.

On the other hand, I am much more likely to fire off a nasty letter or email if a company failed to live up to my expectations.

I found myself having to hold back from doing just that recently when a product I ordered took three weeks to arrive. Turns out the company had shipped it to my billing address rather than the mailing address I provided. I was willing to overlook that – mistakes happen. But what really annoyed me was the company's failure to give me feedback on the status of my package. I was forced to constantly email them and ask for updates. It was like pulling teeth to try to get any information out of them.

This natural human tendency to notice, and comment on, bad behavior, while ignoring good behavior because we just expect it to occur, is one of the terrible twelve training mistakes when applied to our dogs.

Why This Is a Mistake

We have already talked about the dangers of focusing on punishment as the primary or best way to train your dog or change his behavior. The other side of the coin is that if you do not give your dog enough feedback about his good behavior, it will be harder for him to figure it out on his own. Granted, avoiding a bad consequence is a type of reinforcement, but being given something good is a much better idea!

The Mistake: Not recognizing signs of fear and anxiety from your dog.

Years ago, we owned a self-service dog wash from a franchise. As one of our regular customers was drying his dog with the dryer, the dog was sitting on the grooming table, leaning against the wall, yawning repeatedly. Our customer said that was how he could tell his dog really liked his baths, because he was so relaxed during them, he would yawn and almost fall asleep.

Oh my. His dog was anything but relaxed. The reason the dog was leaning against the wall was because he was trying to get as far away from the dryer as possible. He had pulled his ears back against his head, and his tail was tucked tight in a half circle against his legs. Both of these are body postures typical of fearful dogs.

Yawning in this context was not a sign of relaxation. Instead, its what behaviorists call a displacement behavior. These are normal behaviors that are displaced out of their usual context. They are an indication the dog is uncertain and somewhat anxious about what to do. The dog is conflicted about doing one behavior versus another, so to resolve the conflict he does neither. Instead, he chooses a displacement behavior.

In Fido's case, the dog's choices were to jump down off the table (risking the displeasure of and a "correction" from his owner) or stay where he was. As he was trying to decide which was the lesser of two evils for him, he yawned to manage his conflict and anxiety.

Granted, that description is a bit anthropomorphic, but nevertheless the existence of displacement behaviors in conflict situations is well established. And like our customer, most dog owners either do not notice them, misinterpret their meaning, or are not aware such behaviors are extremely important in understanding their dog's behavior.

Recent research bears out our experiences with dog owners. Dr. Michele Wan, a Certified Applied Animal Behaviorist, and our friend and colleague, found that dog owners and professionals with less than 10 years of experience had more trouble identifying signs of fear, stress and anxiety from dogs than did professionals with over 10 years of experience.

Dr. Wan's research* further tells us that regardless of our experience with dogs, people are mostly able to identify when a dog is happy. It is identifying the fear, stress, and anxiety that trips people up. Because most bites occur from fearful dogs, missing these signs can have very bad consequences. At the very least, allowing stress, anxiety, and fear to go unrecognized in our dogs prevents us from either relieving or preventing these conditions, decreases their quality of life, and can even contribute to disease and a variety of behavior problems.

The Reasons People Make This Mistake

Displacement behaviors are a specialized group of behaviors that you would be unlikely to know about unless you had talked to a behavior professional or taken an animal behavior course. Much of the information about canine communication signals that is more easily accessible to the general public in the popular media is either incomplete or just plain wrong. For example, most people have been taught that a wagging tail that indicates a dog is friendly. While a tail that is furiously wagging in a wide sweeping motion is probably a sign of friendliness, a more measured stiff-looking side-to-side wag is part of an offensive threat. But the popular media usually does not tell you that.

Second, there is a real difference between casually watching your dog versus carefully observing his body postures and how they change from moment to moment. And there is also a difference between observing behaviors and interpreting them. You likely have a lot of experience watching your dog's behaviors. Nobody spends more time with your dog than you do. You are best able to notice when her behavior changes because you know what is normal, and typical for her. But you may not always know what features of your dog's body language are more important, or how to interpret what you see. Remember our a self-service dog wash customer and his yawning dog. I'll spend the rest of this part improving your observational skills and tell you the different features of your dog's body to pay attention to, so you will better know when your dog is scared, anxious or stressed.

Conclusion

Thank you for making it through to the end of Puppy Training Basics; let's hope it was informative and able to provide you with all of the tools you need to achieve your goal of training your puppy yourself, without the use of a dog trainer. This can be challenging to do, as it will take a lot of patience and time to properly train your dog. You learned about a variety of topics in this book and learning as much as you can about training your dog can help you to be the best trainer for your dog as possible.

You first learned how to properly prepare for training your puppy. You must start off with preparing for the dog's arrival and make other preparations before training. You must socialize with your dog. You also learned how to avoid critical situations that you may encounter and contribute to. The following topic that you learned about was maintaining control. This is necessary for training, as you must be able to properly command your dog and have them listen to you.

You learned how to avoid common mistakes. There are many ways to improve your training, and it is important to learn about them so that you can avoid making them. After that, you learned about bedtime. It is crucial to know how to handle bedtime so that you and your dog both get enough sleep every night. To continue with training, you can start with basic commands and training your dog to do simple tricks. Doing this can help your dog to be a better listener and follow you better. After that, you learned more about lifestyle training. This included walking your dog and housetraining them. These are important so that your dog can get enough exercise and go to the bathroom properly. You learned about proper playtime with your dog. This is important to create a bond with your dog and allow them the chance to play with you. Finally, you learned some additional tips and tricks to further enhance your training experience and make you better at training your dog. There is always more to learn.

The following step is to use this information and train your dog! It is one thing to know how to train your dog, but it is another thing to actually train them. Keep practicing with your dog every day, and you will soon have a well-trained dog. Never stop learning more about your dog. You must learn how they feel and think, and you will be able to handle them better. You may also keep teaching them more skills. It is crucial to brush up on old skills, too. Try to incorporate everything that you teach your dog into their daily routine, even if it is only for a brief time each day. Your dog will love learning new tricks if you make training fun and reward their good behaviors.

Now that you have everything that you need in Training a puppy now is the right time to start to be a dog trainer. Start your genuine relationship with your pet!

www.ingramcontent.com/pod-product-compliance
Lightning Source LLC
Chambersburg PA
CBHW071909070526
44583CB00016B/1919